Amazing Bullshit

Relax and Swear

Beautiful Critters with Bad Mouths

By
S.B. NOZZL

Copyright © 2016 by S.B. Nozaz

All rights reserved worldwide. No part of this publication may be reproduced or distributed in any form or by any means, mechanical, electronic or stored in a retrieval or database system, without written permission from the copyright holder.

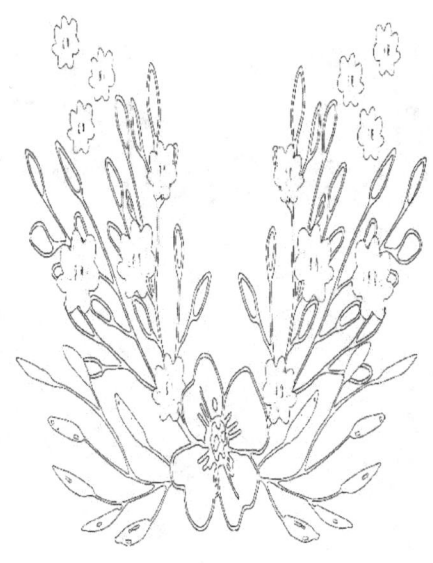

Happy Coloring!

I am in deep shit

I am in deep shit

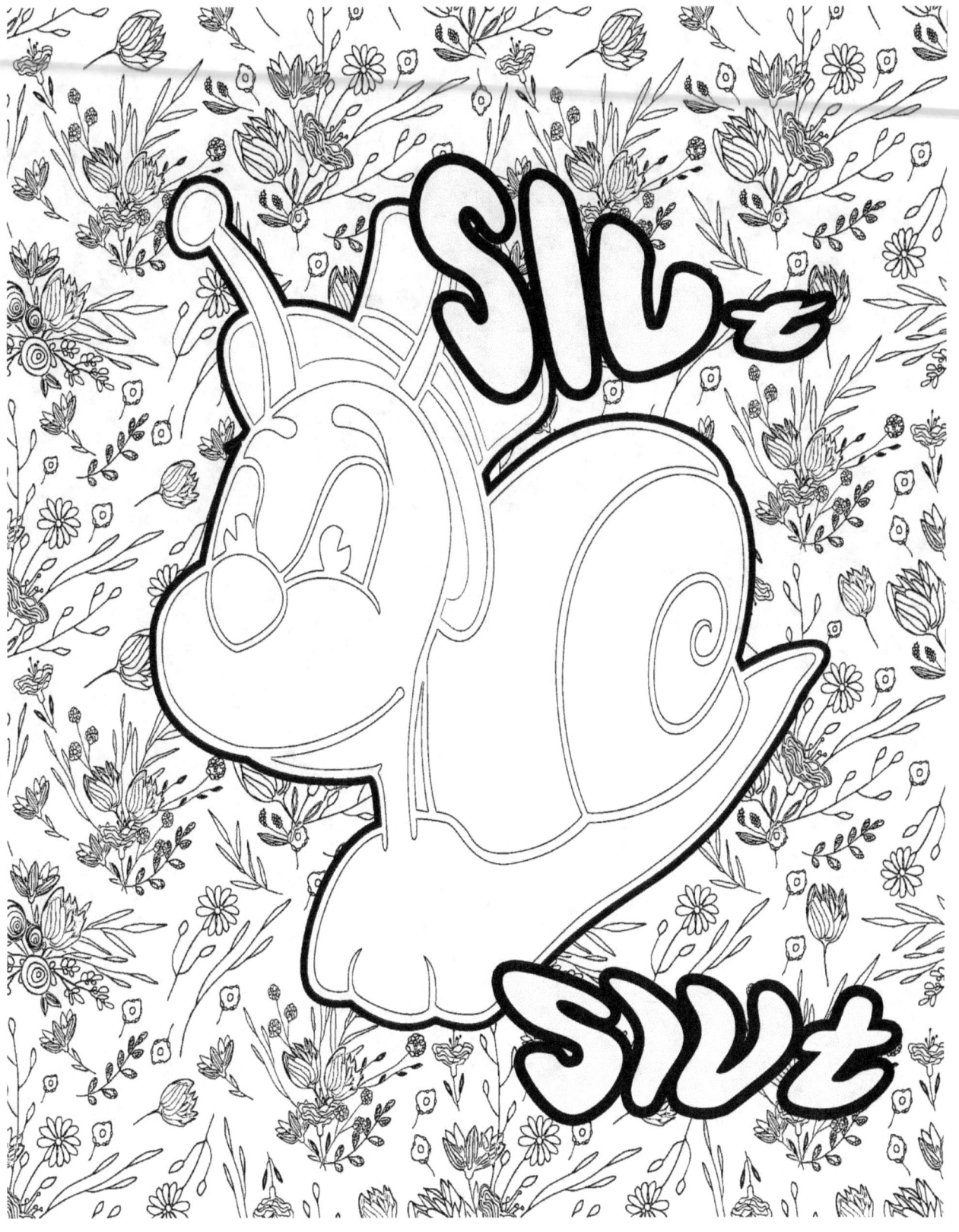

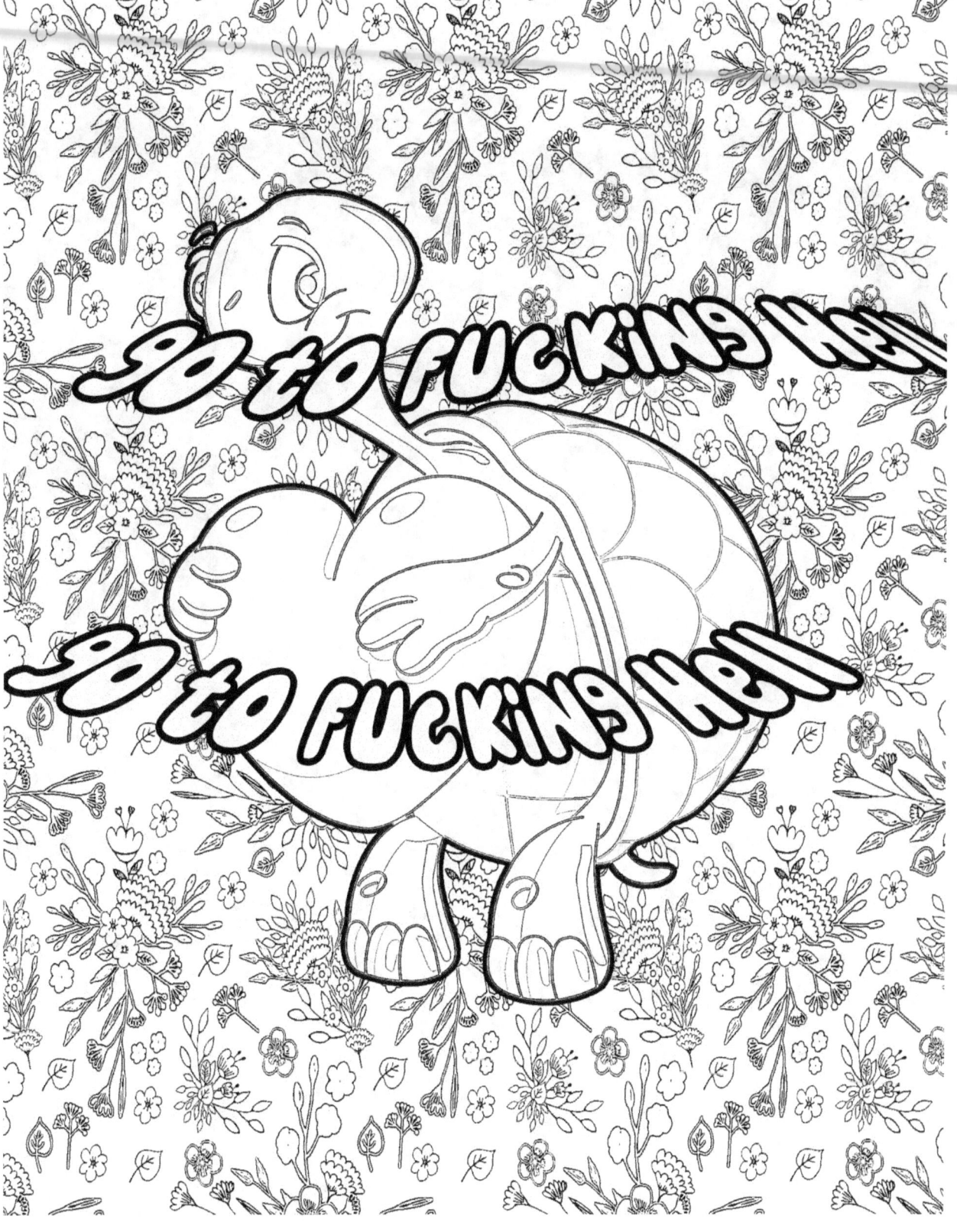

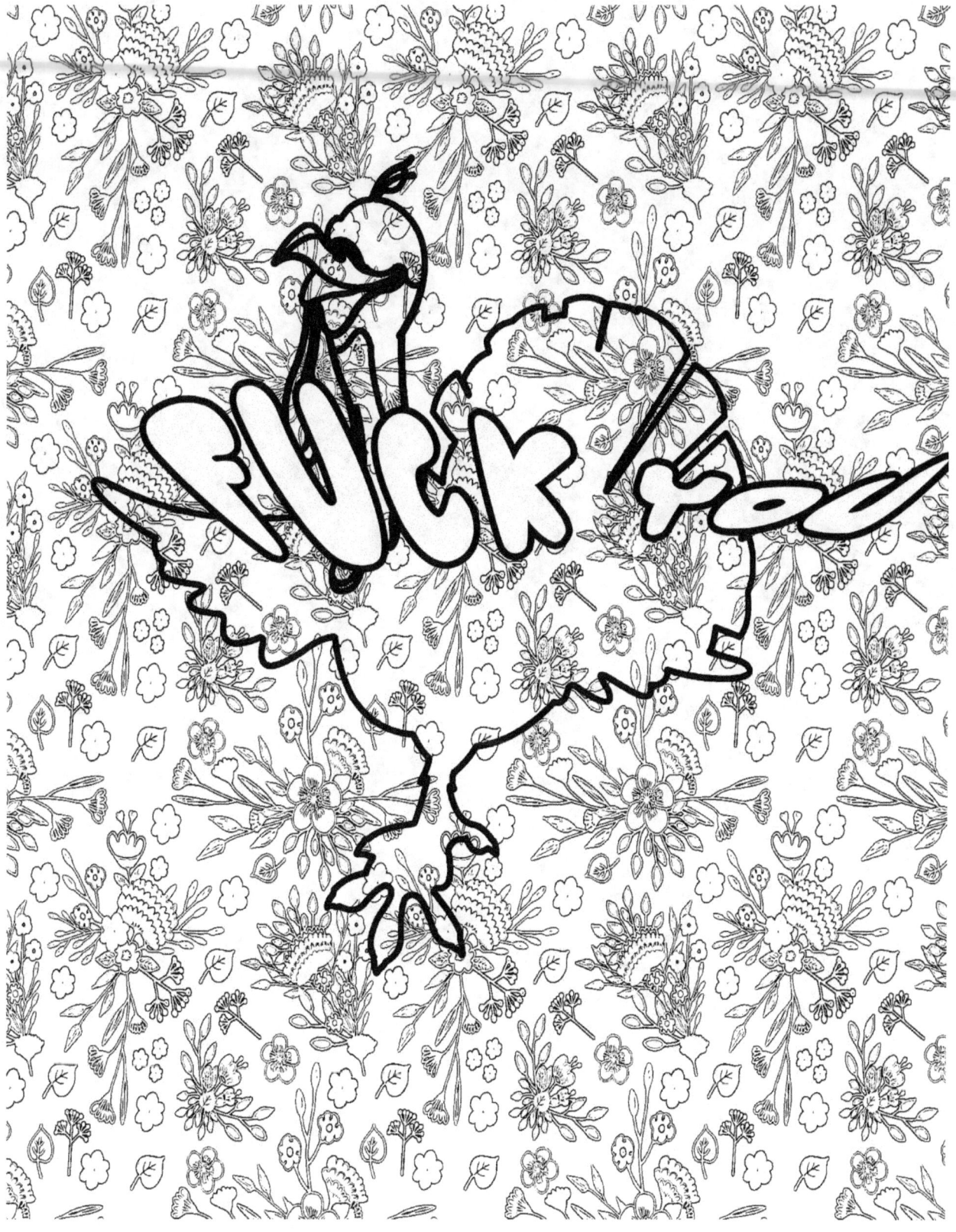

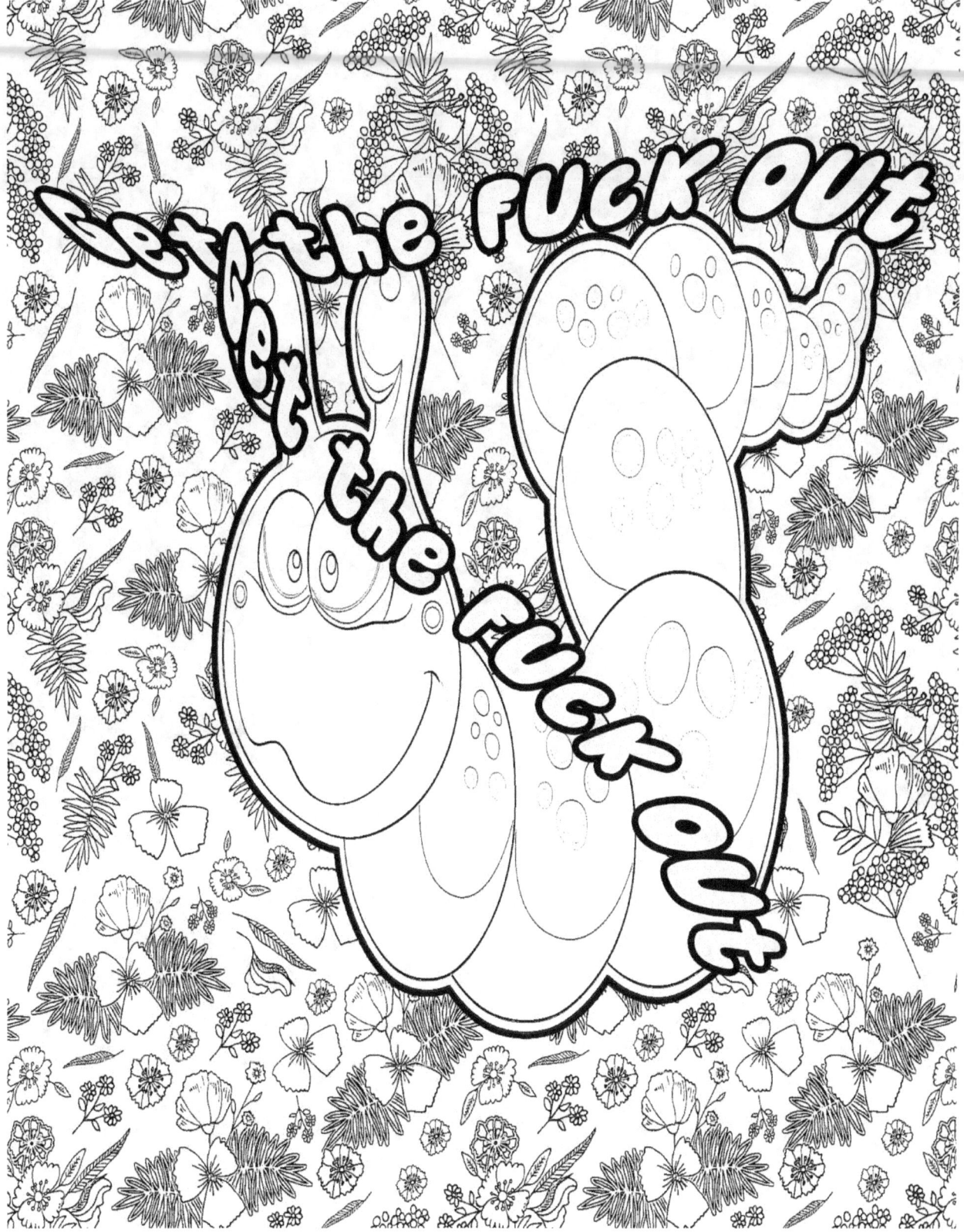

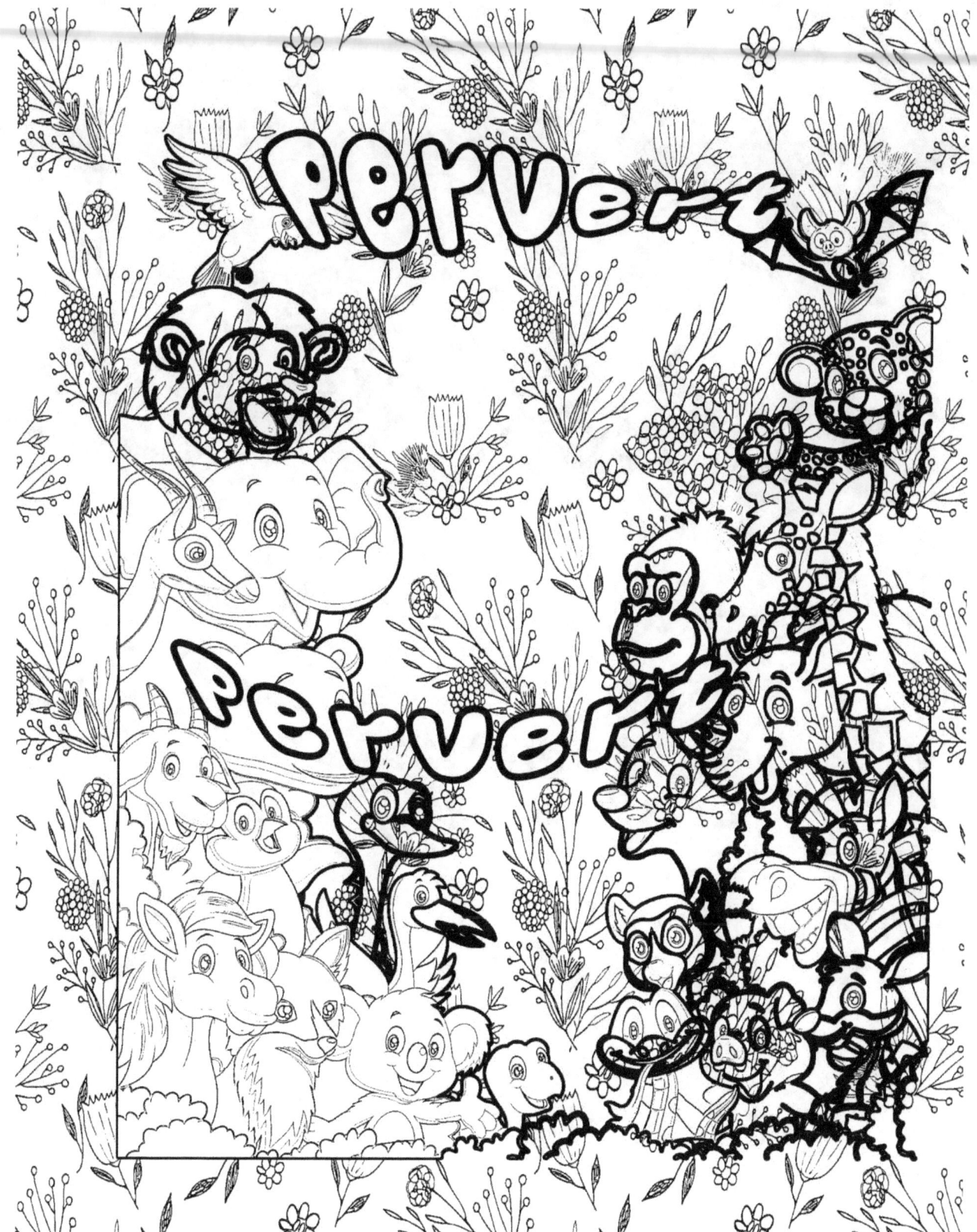

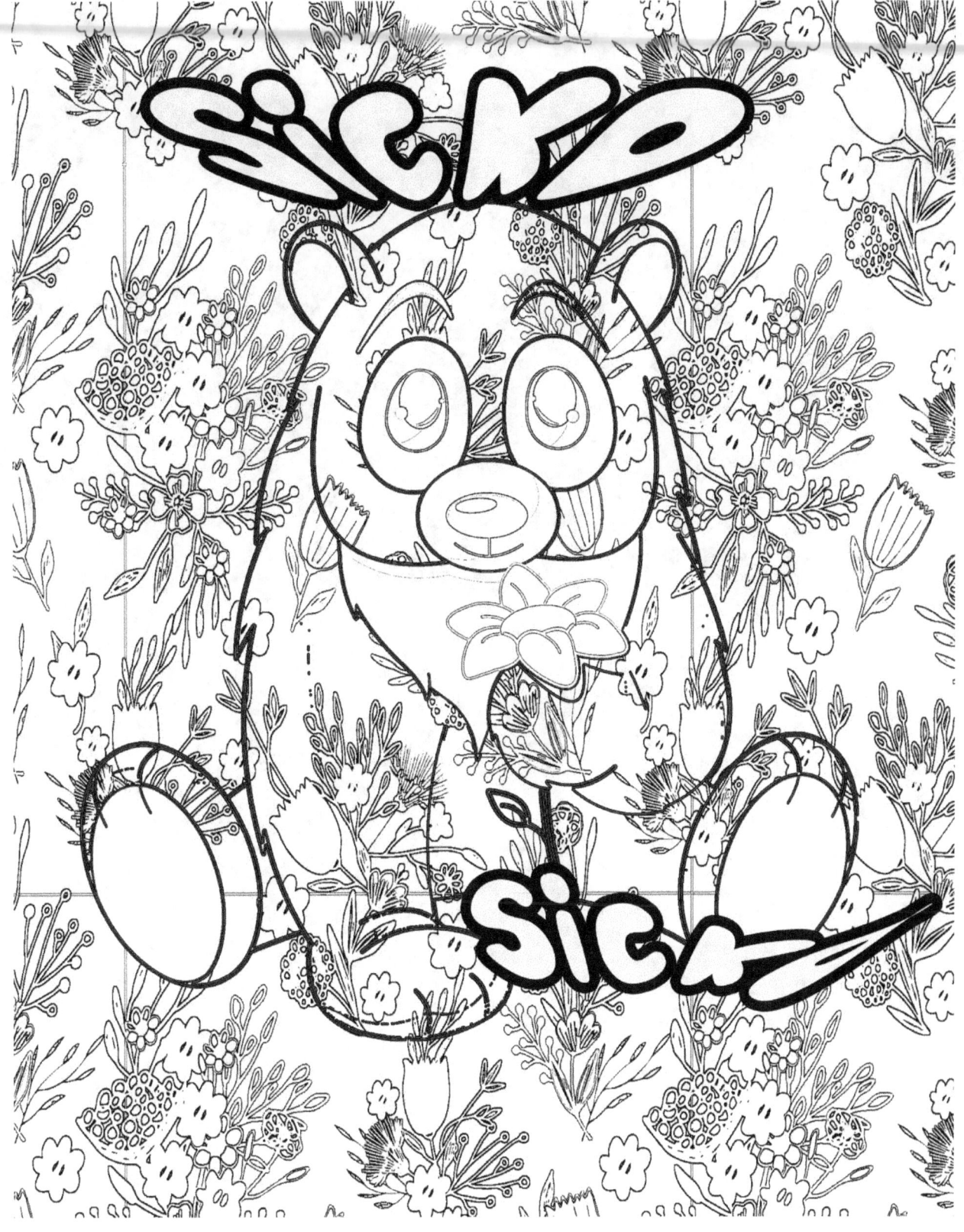

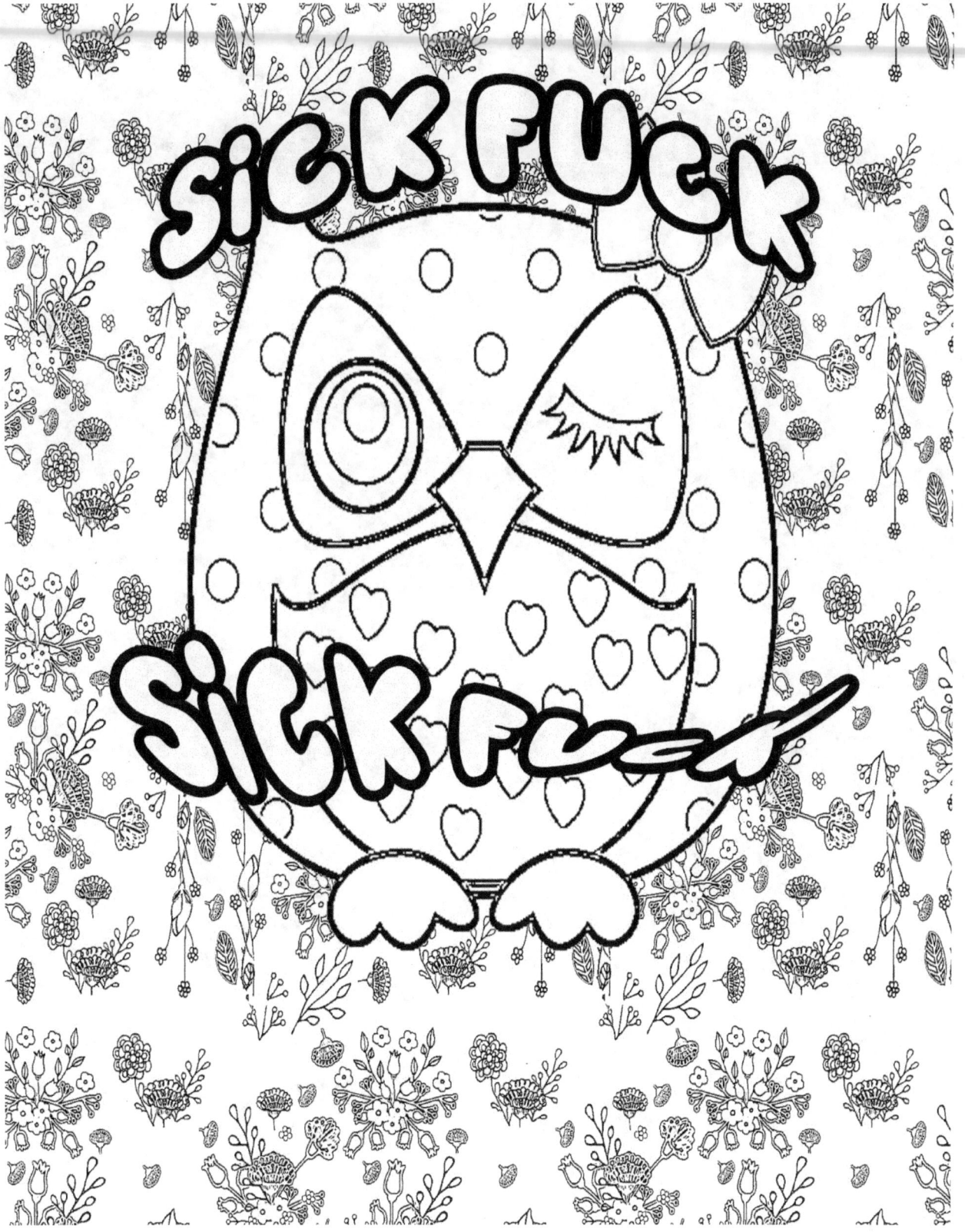

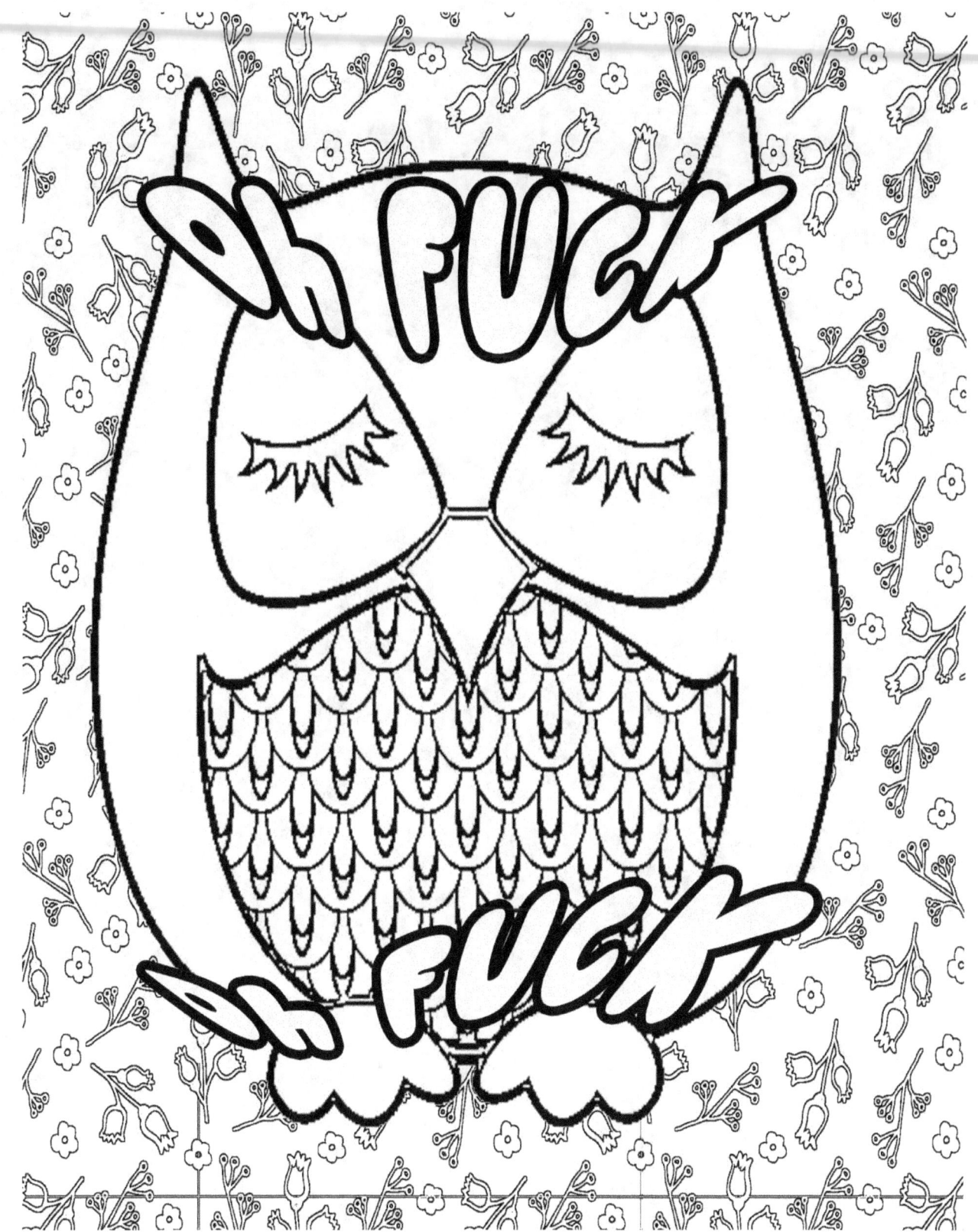

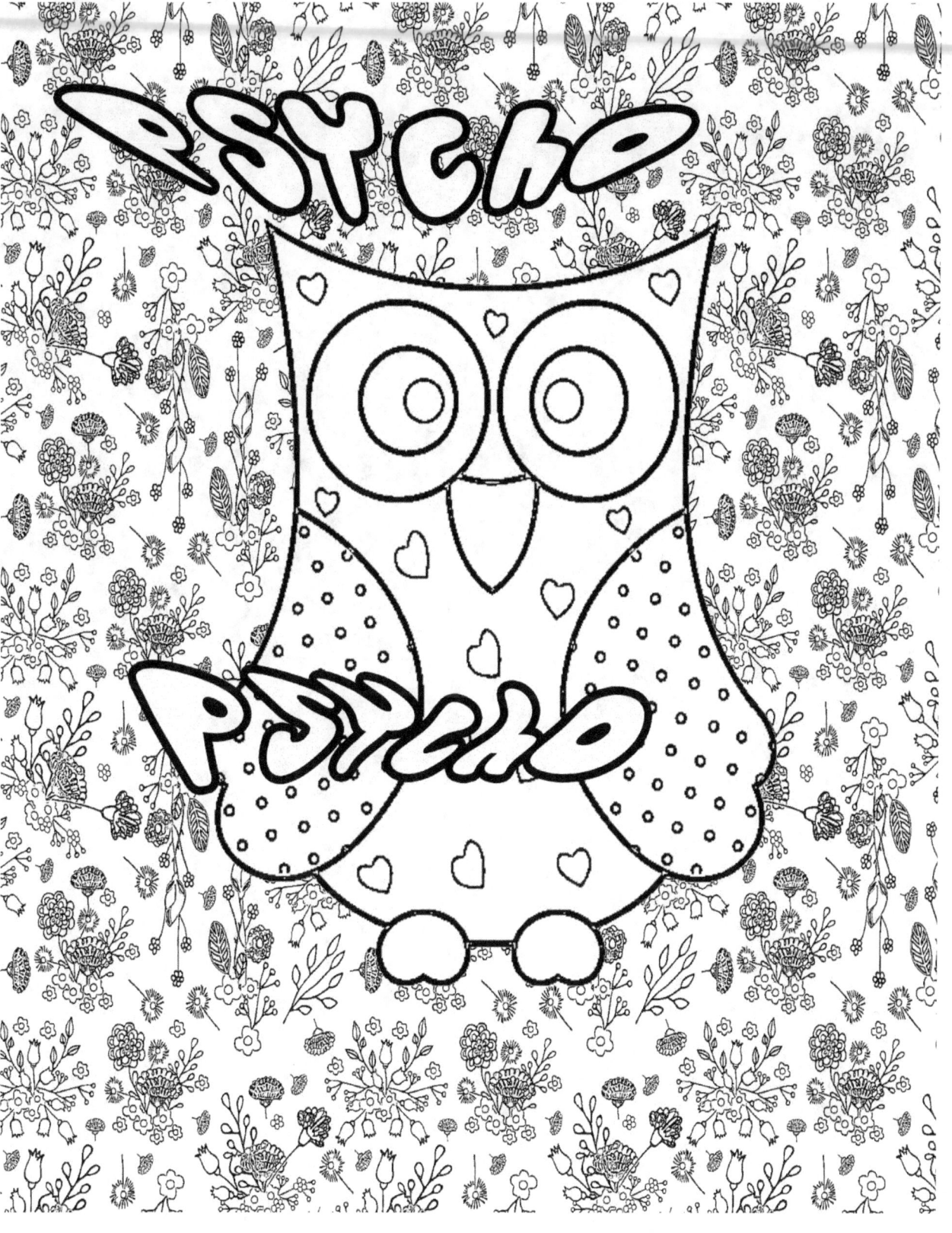

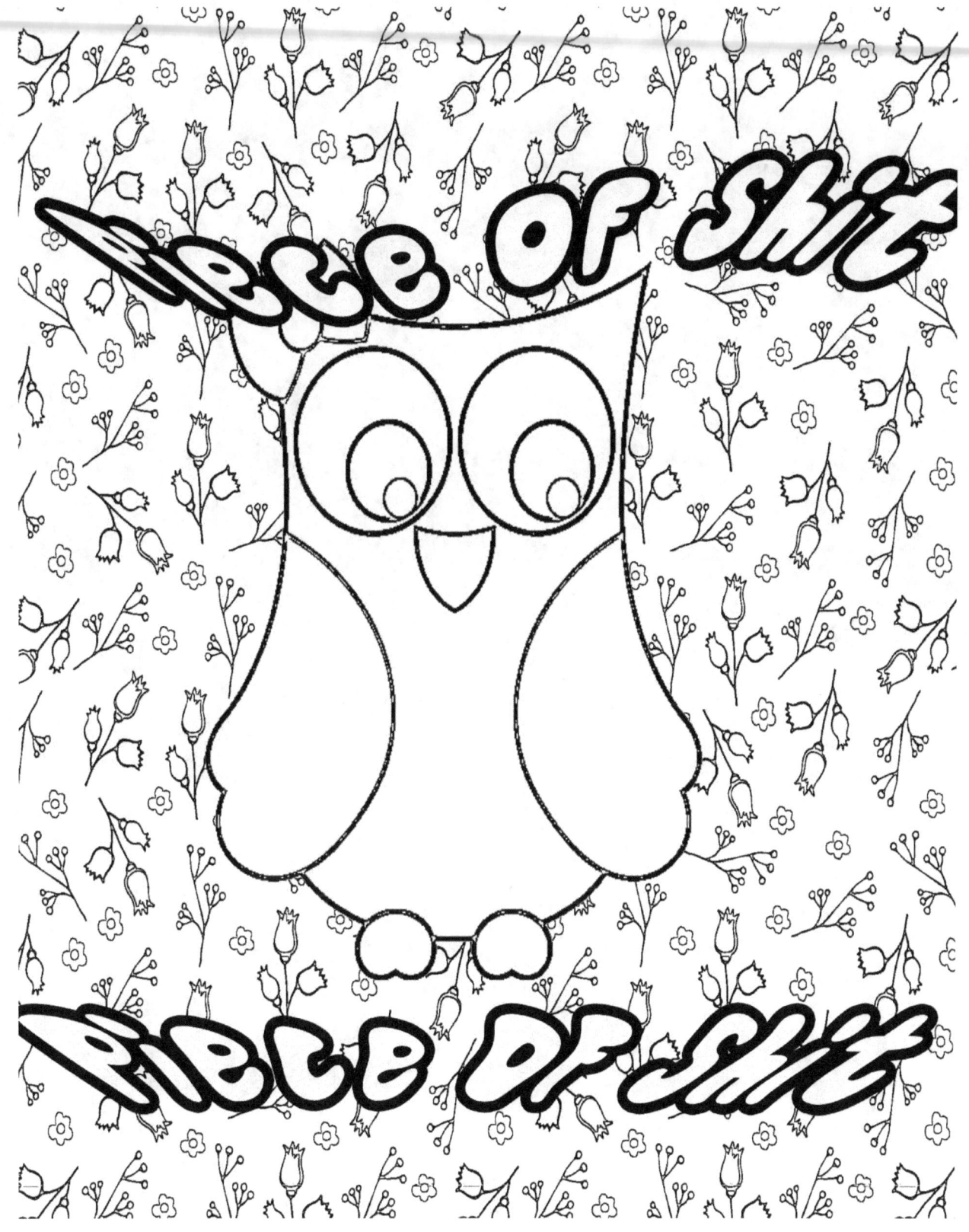

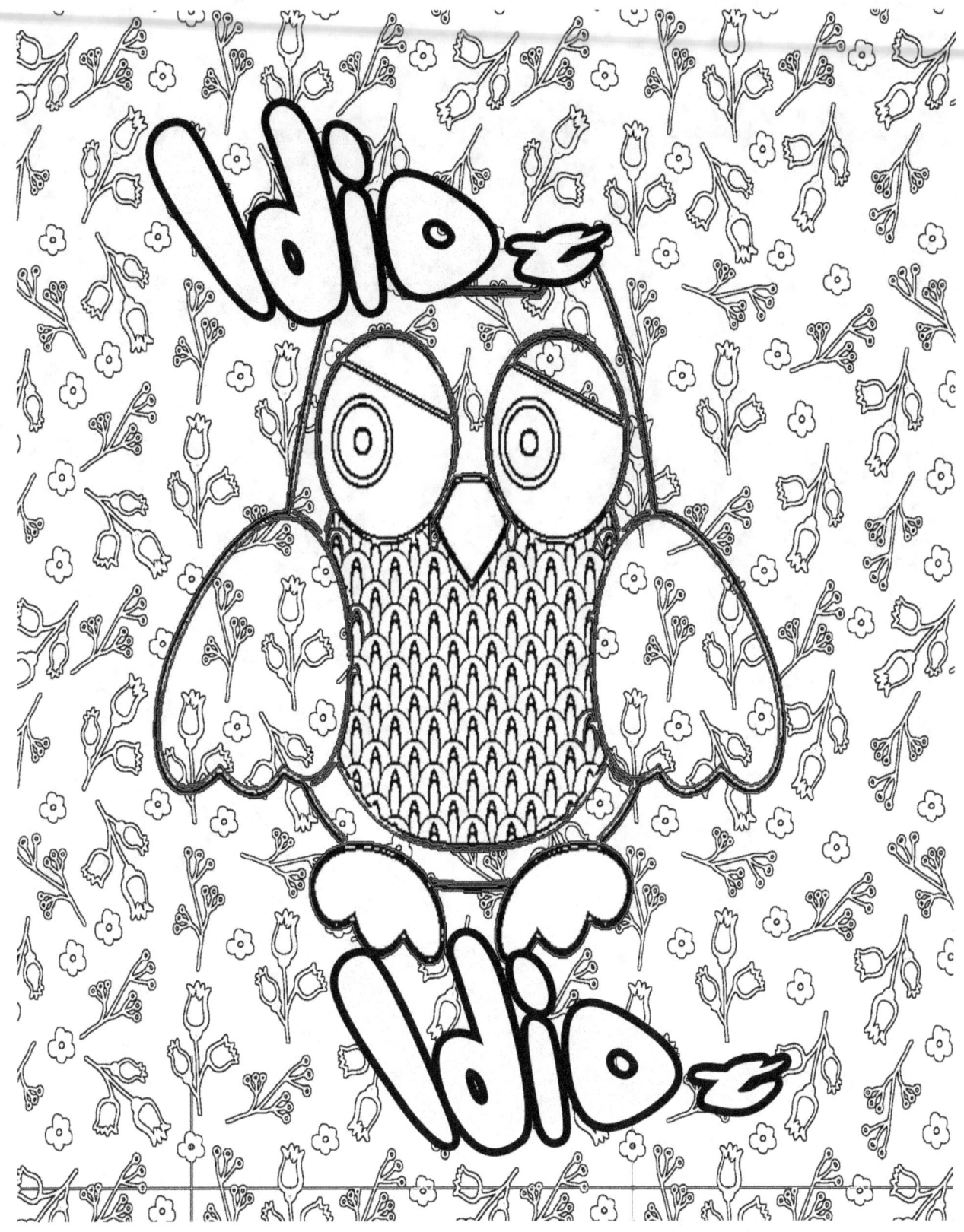

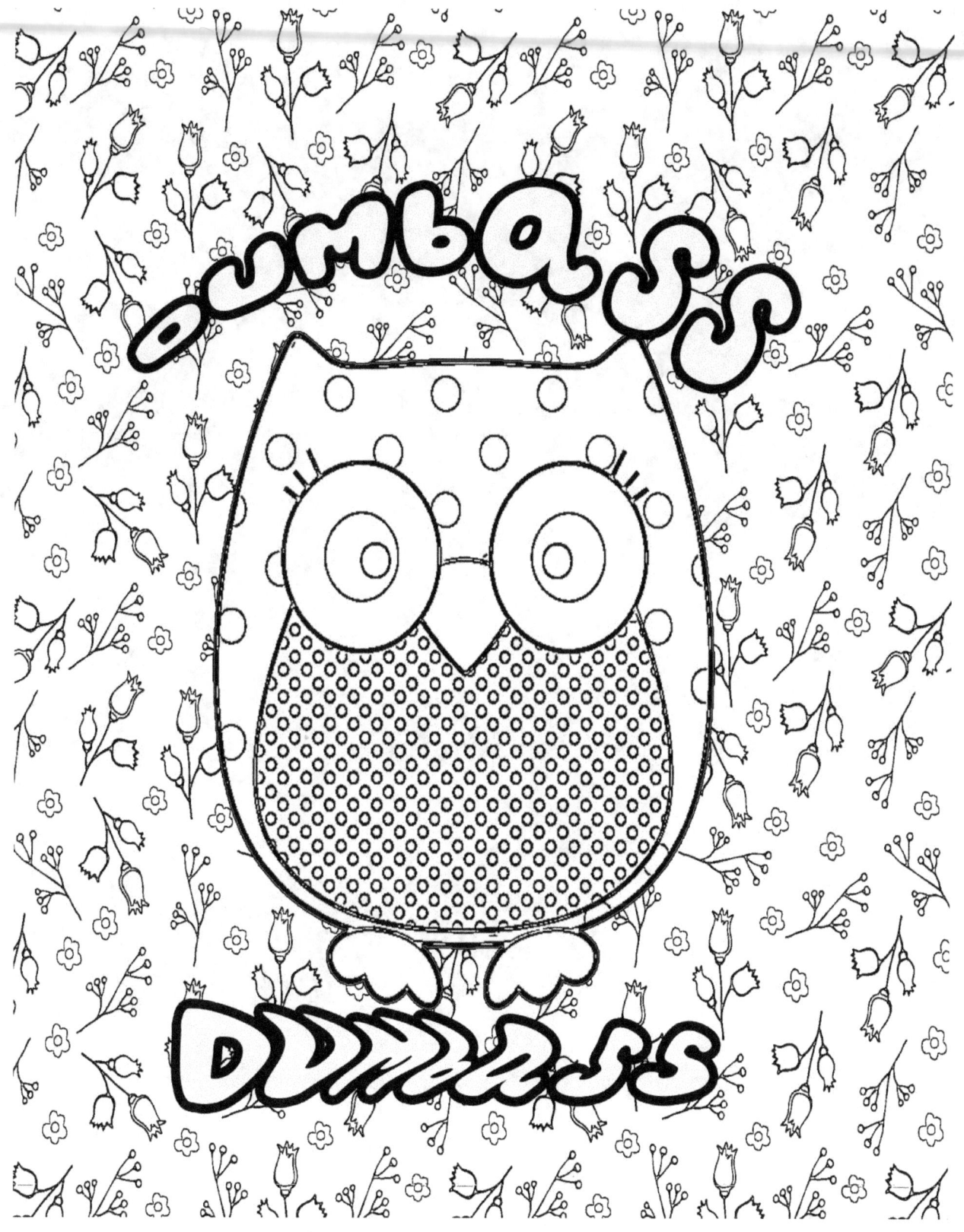

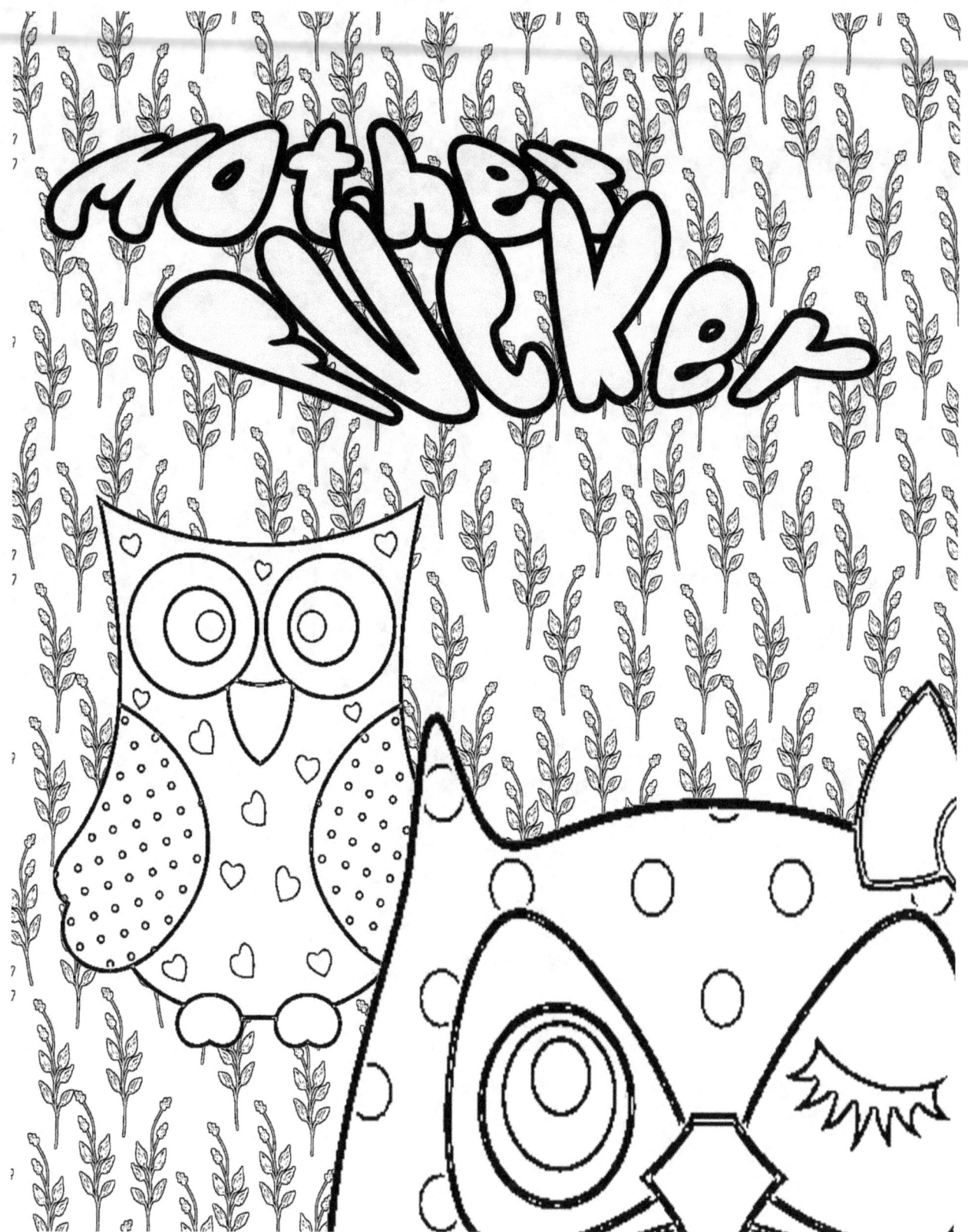

www.ingramcontent.com/pod-product-compliance
Lightning Source LLC
Chambersburg PA
CBHW081125180526
45170CB00008B/3008